ANIMALS GROWING UP™

HOW GIRAFFES GROW UP

Linda Bozzo

Enslow Publishing
101 W. 23rd Street
Suite 240
New York, NY 10011
USA
enslow.com

WORDS TO KNOW

calf A baby giraffe.

camouflage To hide something so it blends in with its surroundings.

cow A female giraffe.

herd A group of giraffes that travel together.

mammals Warm-blooded animals that breathe air, have backbones and hair, and produce milk for their young.

mating Coming together to have babies.

nursing Drinking milk from the mother.

predators Animals that kill and eat other animals to live.

CONTENTS

WORDS TO KNOW 2
LOOK UP 4
BIG BABIES 6
GIRAFFES ARE MAMMALS 8
GIVING BIRTH 10
THE FIRST HOUR 12
PLAYTIME 14
LEAVES FROM TREES 16
KEEPING WATCH 18
NATURAL PREDATORS. 20
A LIFE OF THEIR OWN 22
LEARN MORE. 24
INDEX. 24

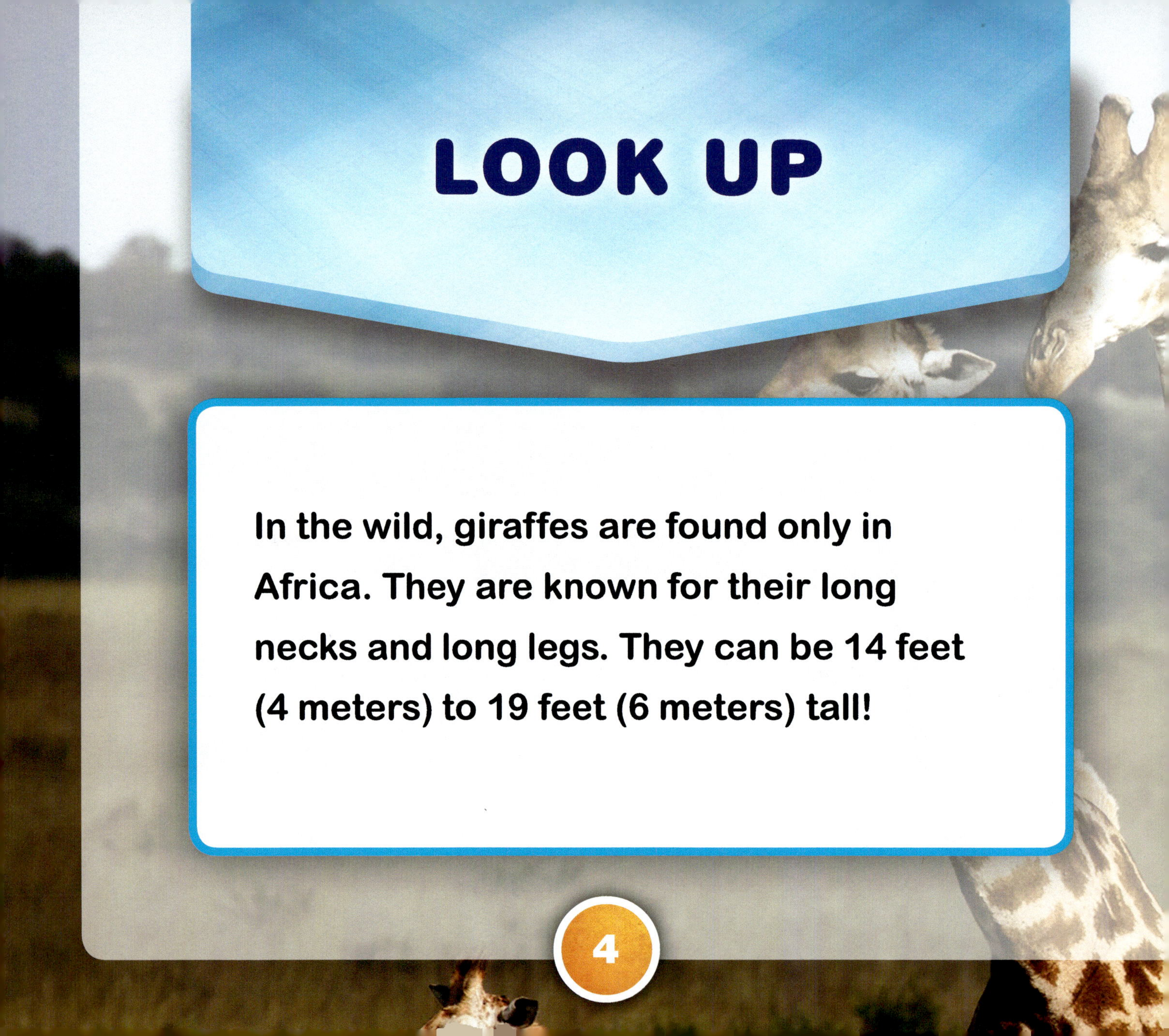

LOOK UP

In the wild, giraffes are found only in Africa. They are known for their long necks and long legs. They can be 14 feet (4 meters) to 19 feet (6 meters) tall!

FAST FACT

Giraffes are the tallest land animal in the world.

A mother giraffe and her baby walk together. They travel across the African plains.

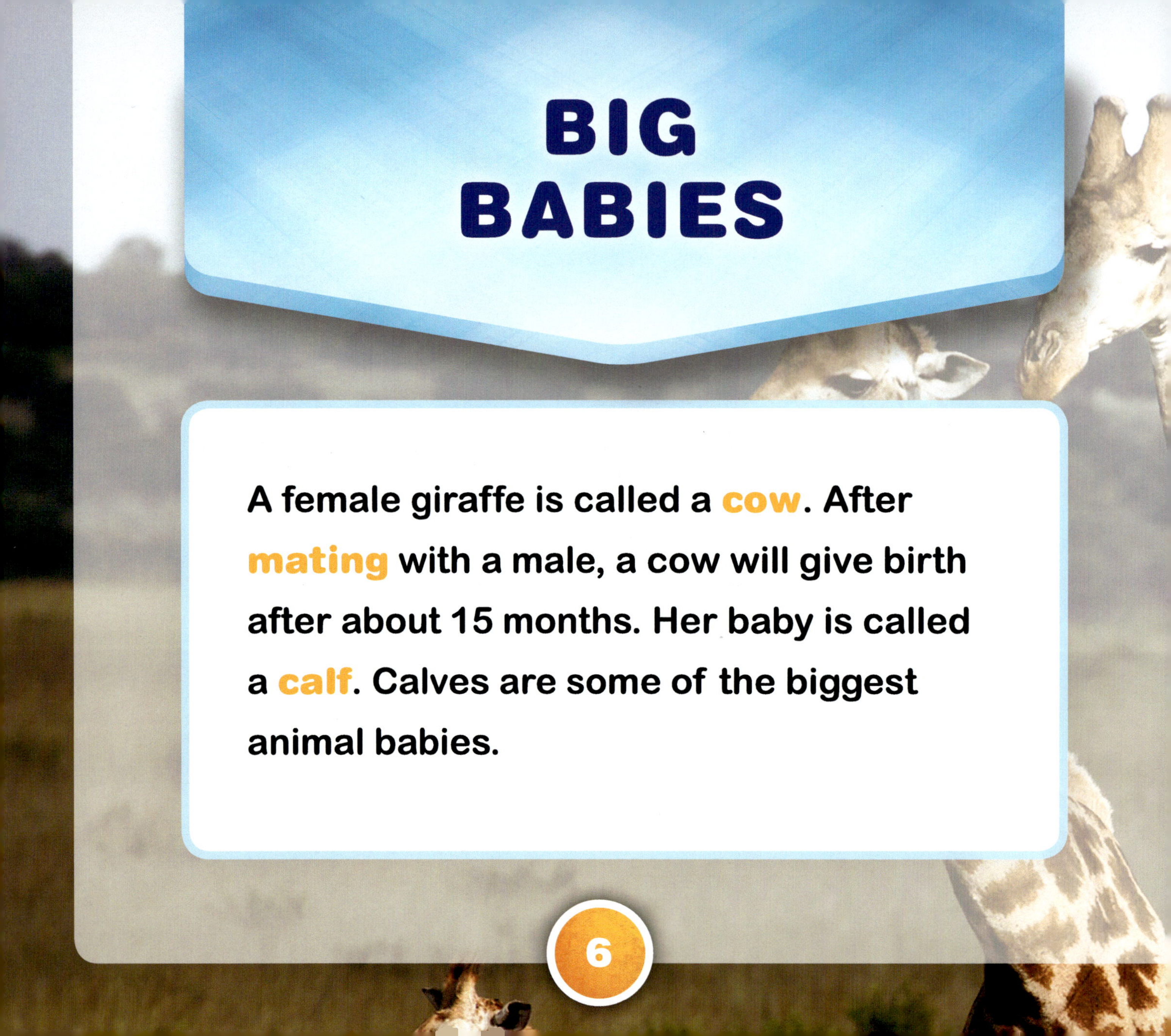

BIG BABIES

A female giraffe is called a **cow**. After **mating** with a male, a cow will give birth after about 15 months. Her baby is called a **calf**. Calves are some of the biggest animal babies.

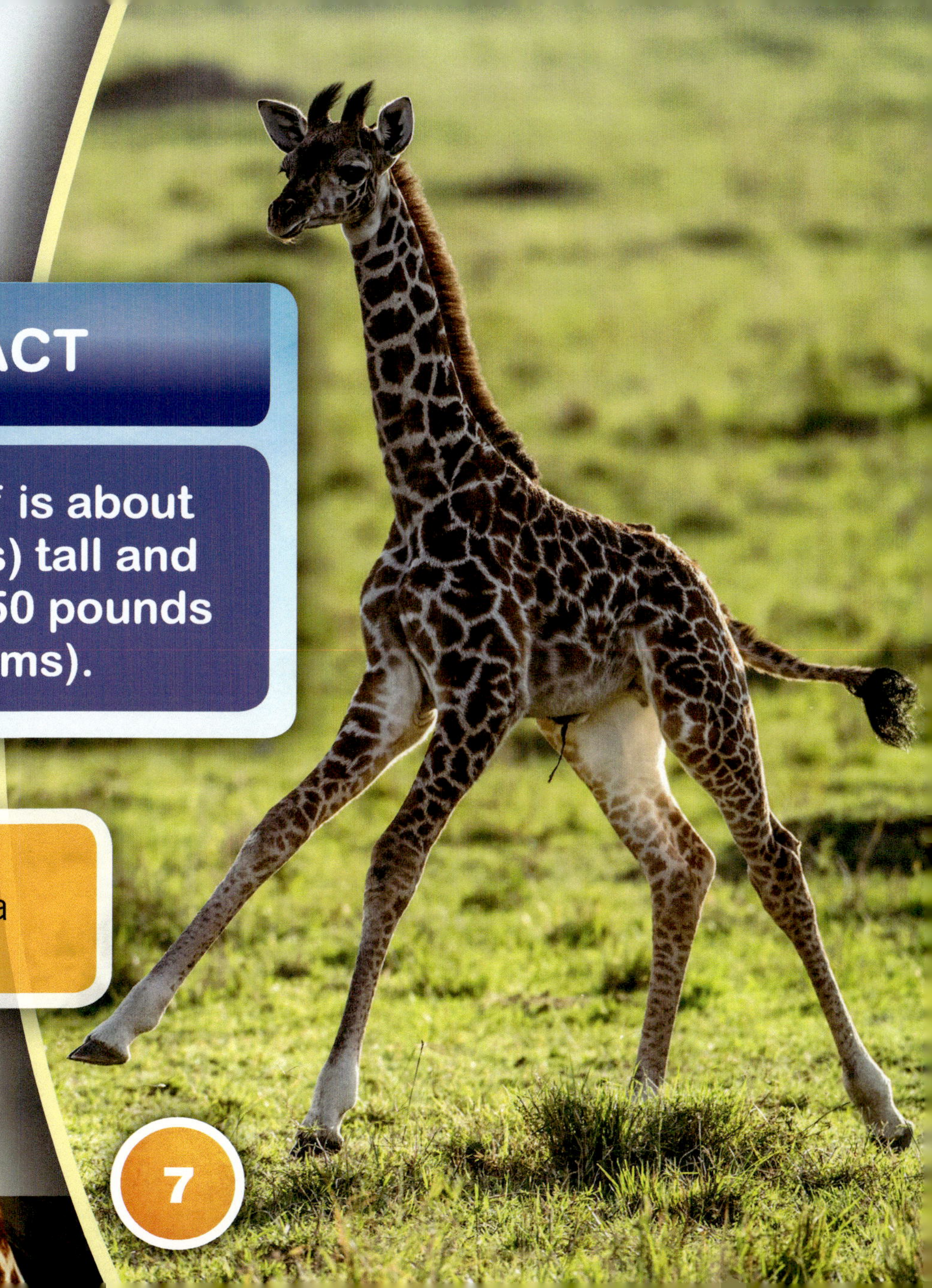

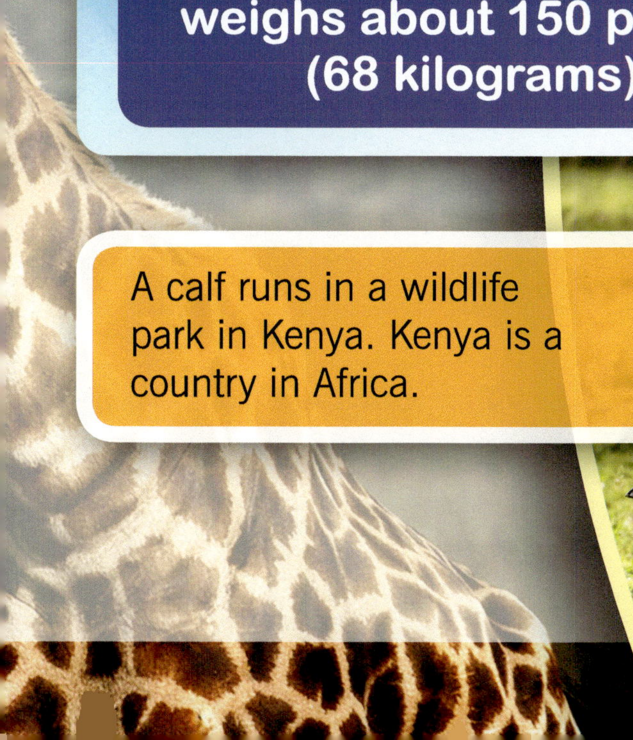

FAST FACT

A newborn calf is about 6 feet (2 meters) tall and weighs about 150 pounds (68 kilograms).

A calf runs in a wildlife park in Kenya. Kenya is a country in Africa.

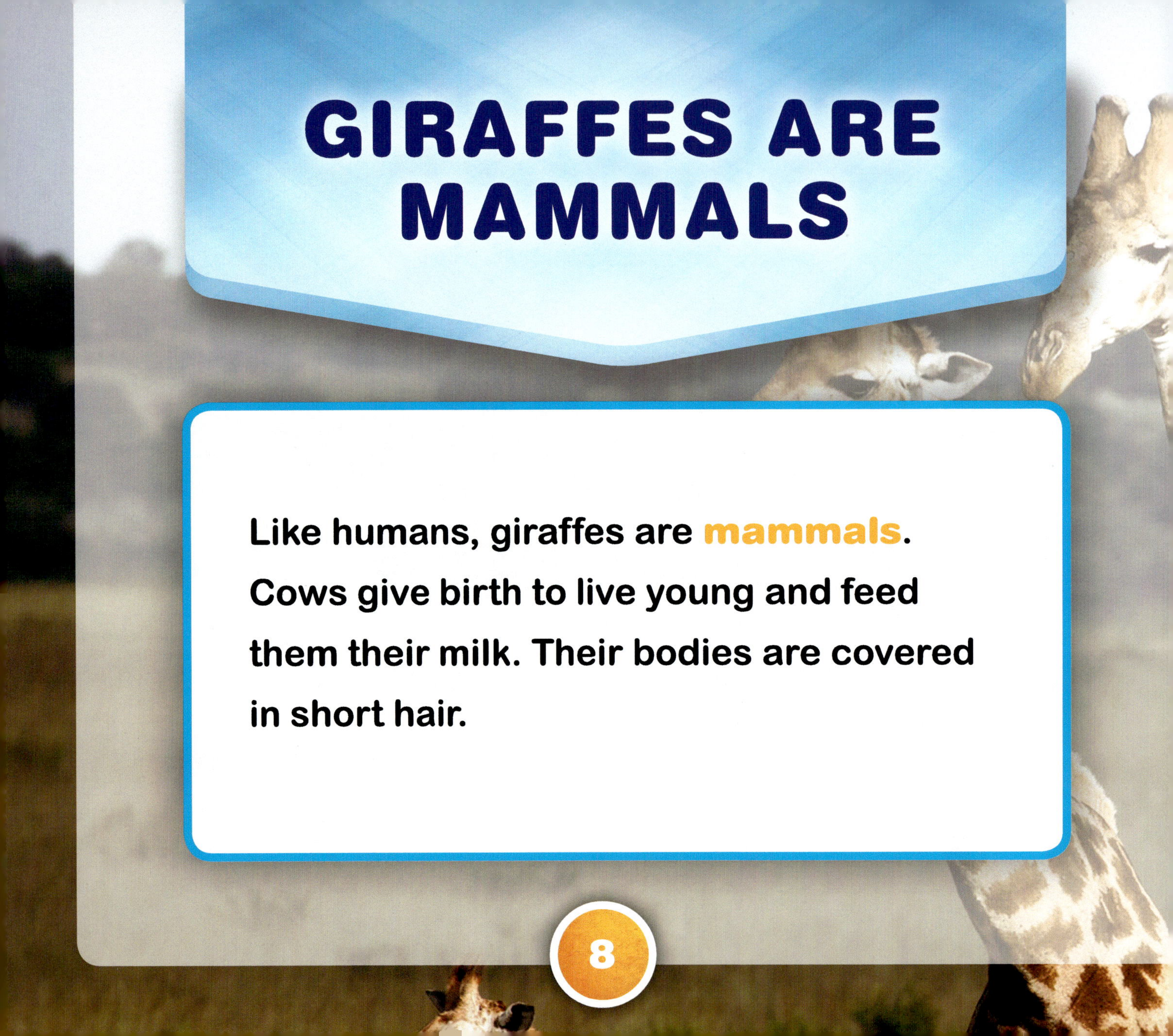

GIRAFFES ARE MAMMALS

Like humans, giraffes are **mammals**. Cows give birth to live young and feed them their milk. Their bodies are covered in short hair.

FAST FACT

Giraffes are born with horns. The horns are covered in hair and skin.

A calf shows off its fuzzy horns.

GIVING BIRTH

A mother cow gives birth standing up. Her calf drops head first around 6 feet (2 meters) to the ground. The fall helps the calf take its first breath.

FAST FACT

The cow gives birth to only one calf. It is rare for a giraffe to give birth to twins.

A cow helps her calf stand up soon after birth.

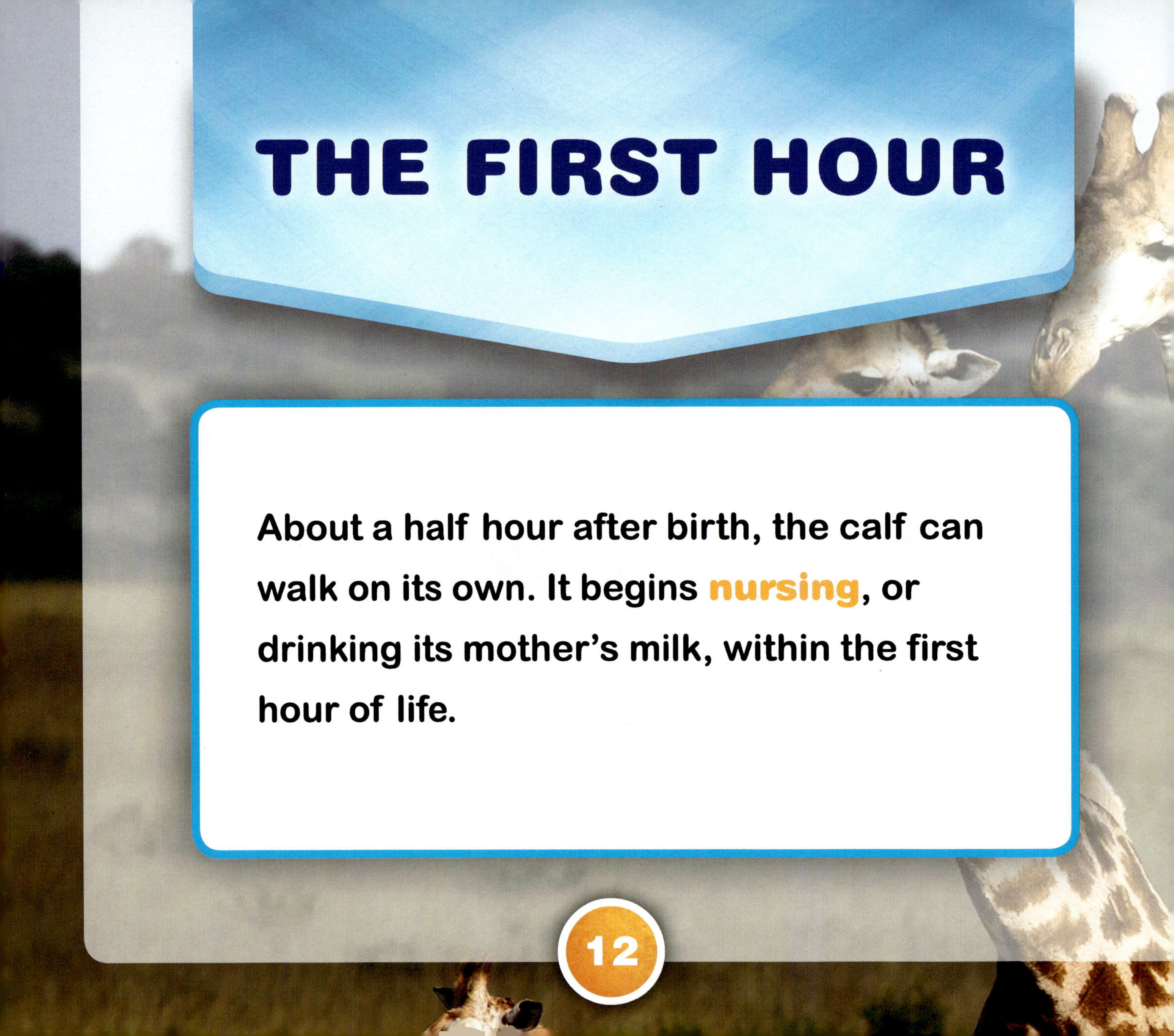

THE FIRST HOUR

About a half hour after birth, the calf can walk on its own. It begins **nursing**, or drinking its mother's milk, within the first hour of life.

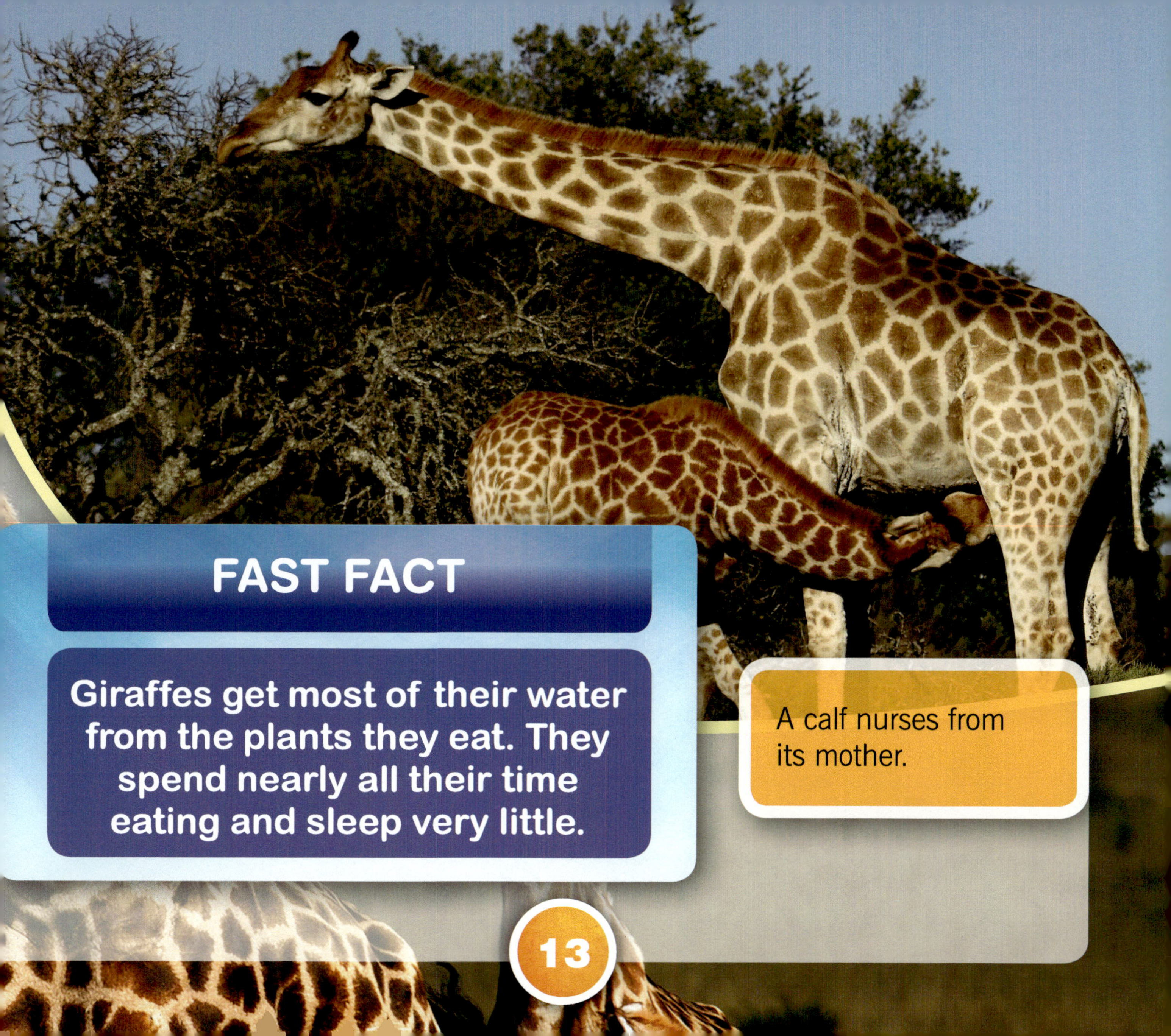

FAST FACT

Giraffes get most of their water from the plants they eat. They spend nearly all their time eating and sleep very little.

A calf nurses from its mother.

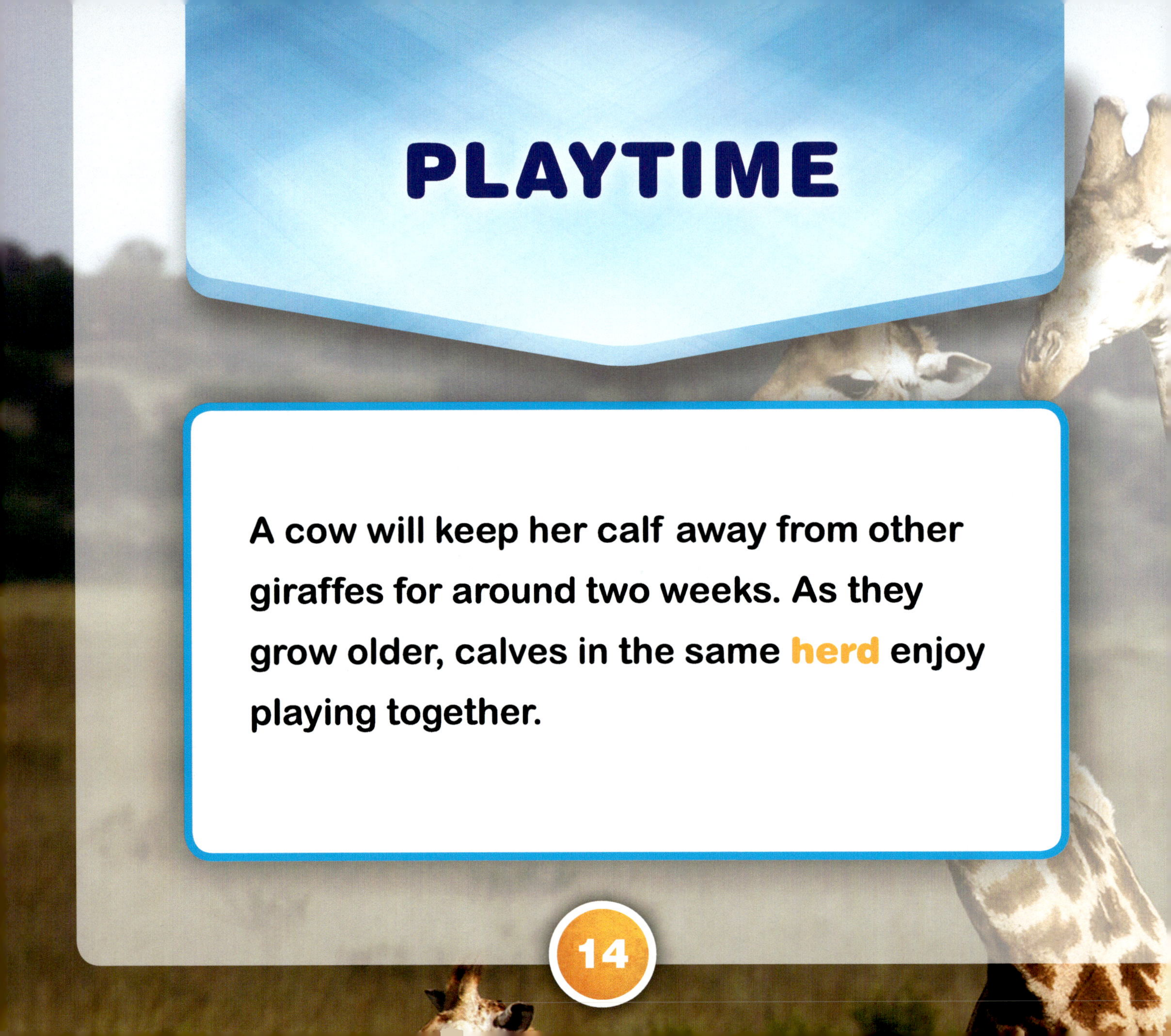

PLAYTIME

A cow will keep her calf away from other giraffes for around two weeks. As they grow older, calves in the same **herd** enjoy playing together.

FAST FACT

The members of the herd change often.

Two calves spend time together in South Africa.

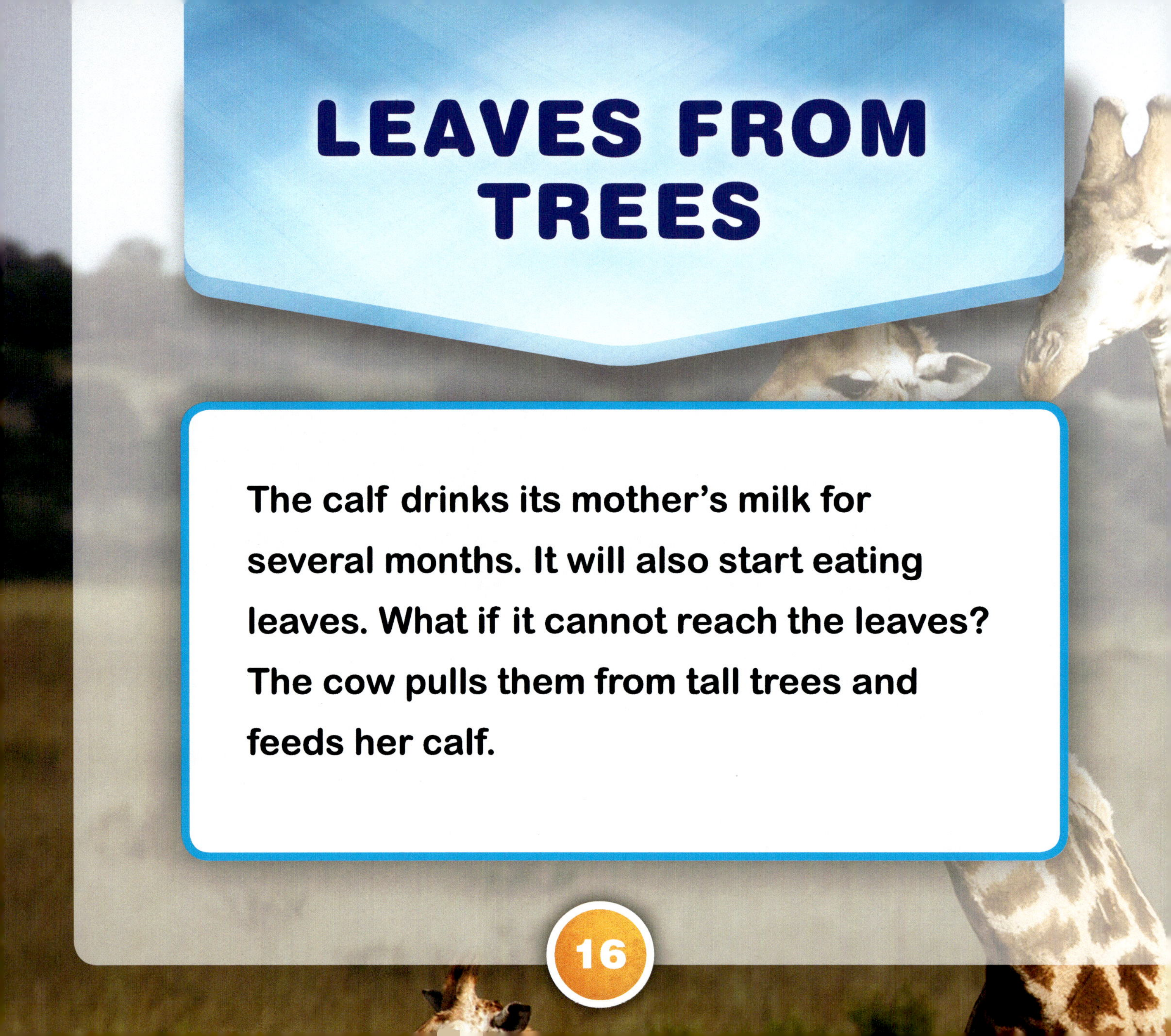

LEAVES FROM TREES

The calf drinks its mother's milk for several months. It will also start eating leaves. What if it cannot reach the leaves? The cow pulls them from tall trees and feeds her calf.

FAST FACT

A baby giraffe's long tongue helps it eat leaves.

A calf munches on leaves from a hanging tree branch.

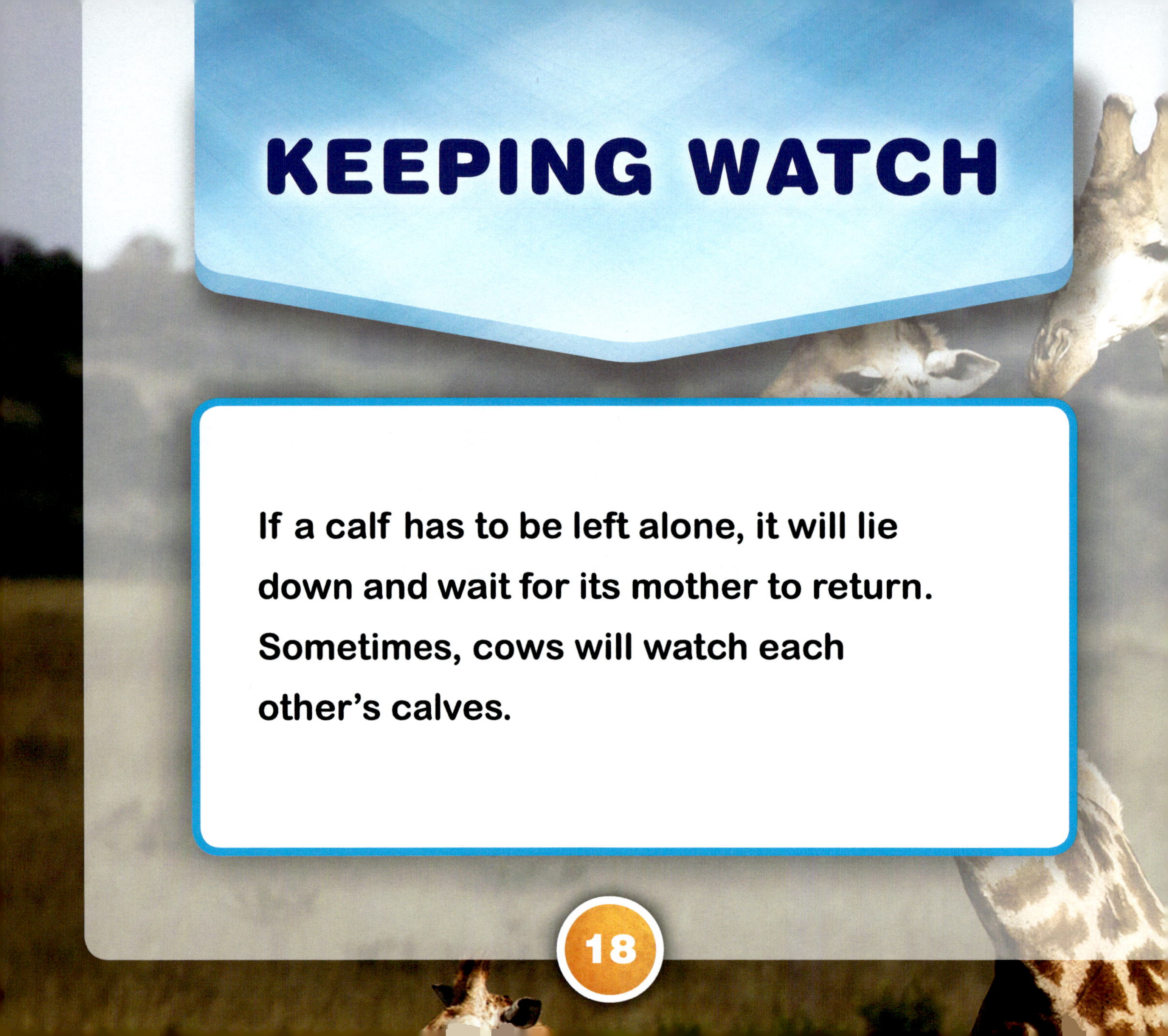

KEEPING WATCH

If a calf has to be left alone, it will lie down and wait for its mother to return. Sometimes, cows will watch each other's calves.

A two-week-old calf hides while its mother eats nearby.

FAST FACT

The cow may leave her calf to go look for food.

NATURAL PREDATORS

Calves rest a lot the first couple of weeks of life. But lying down makes it easy for **predators** to attack. A giraffe's spotted coat helps **camouflage** it from predators.

FAST FACT

Many young giraffes are eaten by predators such as hyenas, lions, leopards, and even crocodiles.

A lion chases after a giraffe. Many calves are lost to hungry predators.

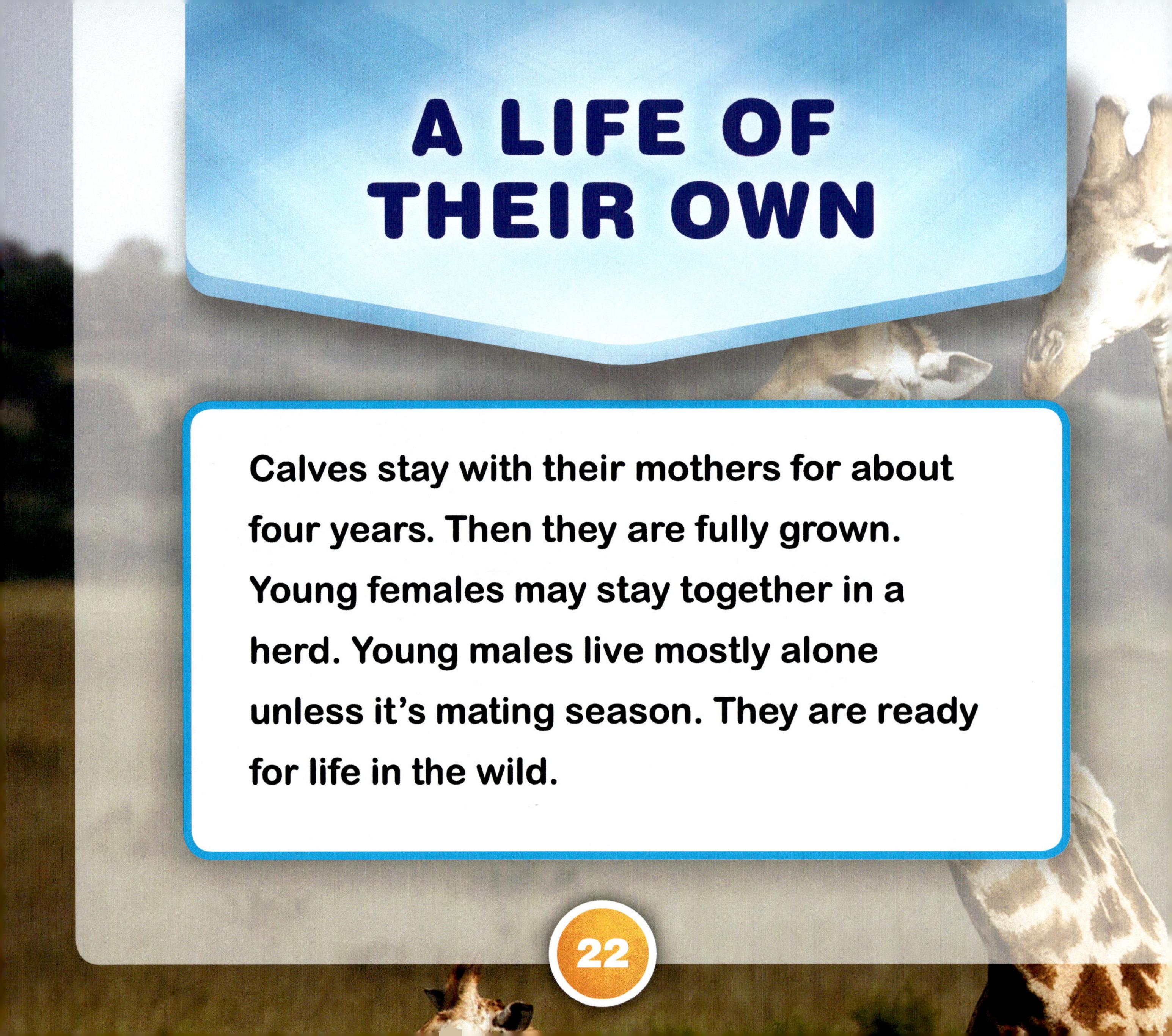

A LIFE OF THEIR OWN

Calves stay with their mothers for about four years. Then they are fully grown. Young females may stay together in a herd. Young males live mostly alone unless it's mating season. They are ready for life in the wild.

Cows are old enough to have their own calves at around four years old.

FAST FACT

Giraffes can live as long as 25 years in the wild.

LEARN MORE

Books

Borgert-Spaniol, Megan. *Baby Giraffes*. Minneapolis, MN: Bellwether Media, 2016.

Hansen, Grace. *Giraffes*. Minneapolis, MN: Abdo Kids, 2017.

Kelley, K. C. *Baby Giraffes*. Mankato, MN: Amicus, 2018.

Websites

National Geographic Kids: Giraffe
kids.nationalgeographic.com/animals/giraffe/
Get the facts on giraffes!

San Diego Zoo Kids: Giraffe
kids.sandiegozoo.org/animals/giraffe
Learn more about the world's tallest land animal, the giraffe.

INDEX

Africa, 4
birth, 6, 8, 10, 11, 12
camouflage, 20
cow, 6, 8, 10, 14, 18, 19
eating, 13, 16, 17, 19
height, 4, 7
herd, 14, 15, 22
horns, 9
leaves, 16, 17
life span, 23
mammal, 8
mating, 6, 22
milk, 8, 16
nursing, 12
plants, 13
playing, 14
predators, 20, 21
walking, 12
water, 13
weight, 7

Published in 2020 by Enslow Publishing, LLC.
101 W. 23rd Street, Suite 240, New York, NY 10011

Library of Congress Cataloging-in-Publication Data

Names: Bozzo, Linda, author.
Title: How giraffes grow up / Linda Bozzo.
Description: New York: Enslow Publishing, 2020. | Series: Animals growing up | Audience: K to Grade 3. | Includes bibliographical references and index.
Identifiers: LCCN 2018044178| ISBN 9781978507210 (library bound) | ISBN 9781978508255 (paperback) | ISBN 9781978508262 (6 pack)
Subjects: LCSH: Giraffe—Development—Juvenile literature. | Giraffe—Infancy—Juvenile literature.
Classification: LCC QL737.U56 B69 2020 | DDC 599.638—dc23
LC record available at https://lccn.loc.gov/2018044178

Printed in the United States of America

Photo Credits: Cover, p. 1 Wansfordphoto/Shutterstock.com; interior pages 4–23 (background), 23 (main photo) Craig Fraser/Shutterstock.com; p. 5 Sergey Novikov/Shutterstock.com; p. 7 Mees Kuiper/Shutterstock.com; p. 9 Awe Inspiring Images/Shutterstock.com; p. 11 © iStockphoto.com/Janugio; p. 13 clickit/Shutterstock.com; p. 15 Jonathan Pledger/Shutterstock.com; p. 17 © iStockphoto.com/stanciuc; p. 19 Jen Watson/Shutterstock.com; p. 21 NaniP/Shutterstock.com; back cover and additional interior pages background graphic 13Imagery/Shutterstock.com.